How to do your PhD: In a nutshell, by
Loizos Heracleous and Najat El Mekkaoui

Published by KDP

© 2018 by Loizos Heracleous and Najat El Mekkaoui

ISBN: 9781980756156

All rights reserved. No portion of this book may be reproduced in any form without permission from the authors

About the authors

Loizos Heracleous is a Professor of Strategy and Organization at Warwick Business School, University of Warwick and an associate fellow at Green Templeton College and the Said Business School at the University of Oxford. More information about his work can be found at his website www.heracleous.org, and on his Twitter feed @Strategizing

Najat El Mekkaoui is a Professor of Economics at PSL Université Paris Dauphine, LEDA-DIAL and a Research Associate at the Smith School of Enterprise and Environment, University of Oxford. More information about her work can be found at http://leda.dauphine.fr/fr/membre/detail-cv/profile/najat-el-mekkaoui-de-freitas.html and at her Twitter feed @NajatMekkaoui

Illustrations by *Telmo Quadros Ferreira*

CONTENTS

So, you always wanted to do a PhD .   5

Chapter 1 – Preparing your research proposal   7

Chapter 2 – The process of conducting your PhD   22

Chapter 3 – Methodological choices and the experimental method .   41

Chapter 4 – Using qualitative methods   53

Chapter 5 – Making a theoretical contribution   71

Chapter 6 – Publishing your work .   91

Appendix – Further reflections on the doctoral process . . .   107

SO, YOU ALWAYS WANTED TO DO A PHD

We are regularly approached by prospective PhD students who would like us to be doctoral advisors for their work. We select on average one doctoral student per year, and do so after careful consideration. A PhD is a long journey, and several things have to come together for the journey to go smoothly and to have a positive outcome.

We realized that often the intensity of the process of conducting a PhD is not appreciated by applicants. Neither are various key considerations, such as how to write a research proposal, select appropriate research methods, understand what a theoretical contribution is, and prepare research for publication.

We therefore decided to write a brief, in-a-nutshell guide on these important aspects of applying for, and conducting a PhD. Each chapter suggests relevant further readings via the footnotes that expand on the points made. We hope that you will find our pointers useful in your own pursuit of a PhD.

CHAPTER 1
PREPARING YOUR RESEARCH PROPOSAL

A journey of a thousand miles must begin with a single step (Chinese philosopher Lao Tzu, 6th Century AD)

Preparing a research proposal is an essential part of the application process to be admitted to a university's doctoral program. Together with other supporting documents such as the application form, your curriculum vitae, your undergraduate and Masters' certificates, and your referee letters, the proposal forms the centerpiece of your application. Prospective doctoral advisors will consider it to decide whether there is a match between their research interests and what you would like to research, and will take the quality of the proposal as an indicator of your commitment to doctoral studies and also as an indicator of your writing competence.

The main parts of the research proposal are: Introduction that sets out the general area of study, including the research question. Literature review, to demonstrate why the research question is relevant and worthy of study. Methodology, where you describe the methods and data you use. Finally, expected contributions of your study to theory and ideally to practice.

Table 1.1. The main parts of the research proposal

Proposal section	Section contents
Introduction	Describes the general theme of the research, with a clear statement of the research question, and why this question is significant
Literature review	Showcases your knowledge of the relevant research, and indicates the research gap that will be addressed by your research question
Methodology	Describes your methodological choices, analytical approach, and the data you will be using to address the research question. See also chapters 3 and 4
Contributions	Describes your expected contributions to theory and also ideally to practice, so that you are able to achieve a PhD and also to publish your work. Includes brief concluding comments. See also chapters 5 and 6

Introduction section

The research question is central and key to the whole design of your research proposal, and the subsequent dissertation. A clear research question facilitates a clear research design and a clear plan for conducting the doctoral research. This question will guide you in structuring the choice of theoretical and empirical models and the dataset that you will use for your analysis. Your research question must be relevant, original, and feasible.

Relevant: Is your research question relevant to existing knowledge on the topic, and to the broader world of practice and policy? You have to establish a clear purpose for your research that is connected to current concerns and debates in the academic field in which you intend to do a doctorate. This explanation would also show why your research question is worthy of being studied, that is, its significance.

Original: The key requirement to being awarded a doctorate is to make an original contribution to knowledge. In order to be able to have a realistic view of whether your idea is original, you have to explore existing research and knowledge on a topic and adjacent topics, have conversations with other researchers and try to think outside the box. This step takes time and you can adjust your initial idea during your work. In chapter 5 on making a theoretical contribution, we discuss such considerations in more depth.

Feasible: Is your research idea implementable and feasible within the 3 or 4-year timeframe you have to conduct your doctorate? Are the data you need to conduct your research available to you, and where fieldwork is involved, will you be able to gain sufficient access to a suitable empirical setting?

Literature Review

Start by looking for papers that offer reviews of the literature in your field. In the management field there are review journals such as the International Journal of Management Reviews, annual issues of the Journal of Management, and papers in the leading theory journal Academy of Management Review. In the economics field, there are review journals as the Journal of Economic Literature and the American Economic Review that can be very helpful in giving an overview of a field.

To identify key papers, you can start the search on Google Scholar or other databases by using keywords, and seeing which papers have a high citation count. These papers are the ones that are more influential in a field and deserve careful attention.

When reading review papers, or recent papers published in high quality journals, pay special attention to the final discussion section, and in particular to the implications for further research. You can see here what are the calls for further research, and anchor your research question accordingly.

Reading the existing literature can be time consuming, and once you start conducting your doctorate you will spend months on this task. For the purposes of preparing the research proposal, you can focus on the most influential papers first, in order to be able to prepare the proposal in a realistic amount of time.

As you carry out your reading, pay special attention to how literature reviews in published papers are structured; how they synthesize and also problematize the existing literature, how they build up to research gaps and identify their research questions.

Methodology

Your methodology must be aligned to your research question. That is, you must use a method that allows you to gain insights and effectively address your research question. There are several methodological approaches in social science that subscribe to different philosophical assumptions (for the example positivist or interpretive paradigms) and involve different ways to gather and evaluate data (for example collecting quantitative or qualitative data and using deductive or inductive analysis, or some combination of the two). In chapters 3 and 4 we expand on methodological choices.

For the purposes of your research proposal, when you read existing literature, you will note that many papers discuss limitations of current research and suggest possible extensions for future research. How could you address these limitations? What sorts of questions or hypotheses remain unanswered or could be analyzed differently? Could you adopt or expand the model or methodological approach used to your own research question?

Your research method will also be shaped by the traditional way in which research questions have been addressed in your field; but do not hesitate to consider other potentially useful methods in related fields. As we discuss in chapter 5, importing a novel method could help you make both a theoretical contribution, by helping you see an existing issue from a new perspective, and also an empirical contribution, by using novel kinds of data or new ways to analyze these data.

Finally, be conscious that your research method must be able to stand up to scrutiny, so it must follow the criteria of robustness associated with the paradigm in which you are conducting your research. For example, a positivist research design must involve clear hypotheses that are testable and falsifiable[1]. Important criteria for an interpretive research design include triangulation, member validation, researcher reflexivity, rich description and an audit trail[2].

Contributions

The path to making a theoretical or empirical contribution starts from the moment you identify a research question. If the research question is based on a gap in the literature and more generally in a gap in the knowledge about a theme, and promises to effectively address that gap, you then have the opportunity to make a contribution. There are several ways to identify gaps in the literature. For example, as we discuss in chapter 5, gaps can exist when empirical research does not support the predictions of a theory; when there are alternative, mutually inconsistent explanations of the same phenomenon; when there is a sense of stagnation or incrementalism in a field; or when research is still at the embryonic stages of an emerging field.

---

[1] Popper, K. 1959. *The logic of scientific discovery*. London: Hutchinson.

[2] Creswell, J. W. & Miller, D. L. 2000. Determining validity in qualitative inquiry. *Theory Into Practice*, 39(3): 124-130.

Your proposed contributions must complement current research

Once you are accepted into a PhD program, discussion with your doctoral advisor would be essential in helping you frame your research proposal and then carry out your research so that it can effectively address a worthwhile research gap.

It is important to be focused when trying to make a theoretical or empirical contribution. This process involves a balancing act however. If you are too narrow, your attempted contributions may be too esoteric or trivial. If you are too broad, your attempted contributions will be too superficial. Framing contributions involves practice and experience. The more published academic papers you read, if you read them consciously and with attention to how they frame their contributions, the more your understanding will advance. Also, it would be helpful to read carefully some targeted papers on what a theoretical contribution is, and how to make one[3]. Throughout the book, the references in the footnotes will help you expand your reading in these and other areas.

Research potential doctoral advisors

When you prepare your research proposal, you may have to approach prospective doctoral advisors. Advisors tend to select doctoral students who would like to research themes that are consistent with the advisor's research interests. Take the time to explore prospective advisors' webpages, see what themes they research and what they have published, and try to inform your research proposal accordingly. When you contact prospective advisors, tailor your message so that they can see that you are aware what their fields of research are, and that you have reflected on why they would be suitable advisors to supervise your study.

---

[3] Corley K. G. & Gioia, D. A. 2011. Building theory about theory building. What constitutes a theoretical contribution? *Academy of Management Review*, 36: 12-32; Locke, K. & Golden-Biddle, K. 1997. Constructing opportunities for contribution: Structuring intertextual coherence and "problematizing" in organizational studies. Academy of Management Journal, 40: 1023-1062; Whetten, D. A. 1989. What constitutes a theoretical contribution? *Academy of Management Review,* 14: 490–495. Barberis, N. C. 2013. Thirty Years of Prospect Theory in Economics: A Review and Assessment. *Journal of Economic Perspectives*, 27(1): 173-96.

Learn about potential doctoral advisors and customize your approach to them

It would be useful to understand what Professors look for in prospective doctoral candidates. Boxes 1.1 and 1.2 below offer some insight on this.

> **Box 1.1. What I look for in a prospective PhD student**
>
> Undertaking a doctoral study requires a lot of commitment in terms of time and effort. Those who carry out such life-changing journey tend to exhibit, from the outset, a set of attributes that can enable them to both complete and enjoy this journey. These are the exact attributes I seek when considering prospective PhD students, as these will enable them to complete their journey, enjoy it and build the bases for their future

careers. So, what are these attributes?

First, an excellent academic record from a reputable institution that demonstrates the candidate has mastered important academic skillsets, like carrying out a comprehensive literature review or critically evaluating the findings of studies, which will be critical during their doctoral research. Second, evidence of immersion in the particular topic and method the candidate wants to explore. For example, if the candidate writes in their proposal that they want to employ interviews for their data collection, it is important that they have had some prior experience of qualitative methods. If they want to study a particular industry, some level of experience of that industry, or a related one, is often useful. Third, potential to become independent thinkers so they can push our knowledge forward by conducting a cutting-edge study based on the highest professional standards. I seek out this potential for independent thinking when evaluating their application, proposal, academic record and when having interviews with them. The above three attributes are the ingredients for a successful PhD journey ahead.

Sotirios Paroutis is Professor of Strategic Management at Warwick Business School.

> **Box 1.2. What I look for in a prospective PhD student**
>
> Choosing a new PhD student is always a big risk. Professors will potentially be spending countless hours over several years with this person and reading his/her work, so it is important that there is a good fit! I look for students who can show that they are able to write well, and who have a track record of delivering on commitments.
>
> While a fully developed research idea is not necessary at the start of the process, it is helpful to have at least begun thinking through a research idea and its implications. If a student is interested in at least some of the same theories as I am, the possibilities of having a mutually productive supervisory relationship increase dramatically. Finally, I look for students who are able to work with constructive feedback. Academic life is built on our ability to provide and accept reviews of each other's work, and life is easier for everyone if a new student is able to respond effectively and adapt to constructive suggestions.
>
> *David Oliver is Senior Lecturer in Work and Organization Studies at the University of Sydney.*

The Table below summarizes the steps for preparing a research proposal. Bear in mind that these are not always linear, you may have to back and forth the various stages until you feel satisfied that you have a viable research idea and a high quality research proposal.

Table 1.2. Steps for preparing a research proposal

Step	Description
Provisional Theme	Think of some options or a general idea of what you would like to research, that you can then narrow down as your reading advances
Read literature	Start reading the relevant literature, particularly good literature review papers. Search Google Scholar or other databases, paying attention to which papers have the highest citation counts, and are therefore central to a discipline
Decide research question	As your reading advances, and you have a better idea of the literature in a field, narrow down and focus your theme, in terms of a research question. Base your choice of research question on a gap indicated by the literature you have read
Decide on methodology	Reflect on what particular methods and dataset would be appropriate to use for your research. Make a decision on inductive or deductive approaches (or a mixture), and then decide which particular methods within these approaches you will use
Reflect on contributions	Spend some time thinking about what the potential contributions of your research will be, in relation to the research question you have selected.

	Think of theoretical and applied contributions
Prepare research proposal	Using the outputs of the above steps, prepare your research proposal. Include introduction, literature review, methodology, and contribution chapters
Search for doctoral advisor	Do your research on who would be a suitable doctoral advisor, look at their webpage, see what research they have done, and tailor your message to them when you get in touch
Make formal applications to Universities	Gather all the paperwork needed, and make formal applications to Universities. Try to include all relevant paperwork with a high quality research proposal, as Universities and prospective advisors get many applications and the competition for acceptance is intense

CHAPTER 2
THE PROCESS OF CONDUCTING YOUR PHD

You have 3 to 4 years to complete your PhD, depending on the particular country you are in, the nature of your funding, and whether you engage in teaching or other work during your doctoral studies. Even though 3 to 4 years sounds like a lot of time, when you compare this with the magnitude of what you have to produce, it will feel like the time is moving fast. If you spend too long on a particular stage of your PhD, you may find that you feel squeezed and short of time in subsequent stages.

Therefore, it is important to plan your time carefully and to try and follow your plan (with reasonable allowance for any changes in direction or any contingencies). Often the first year of your doctoral studies will involve classes in theory and methodology. During this time period you will also be reading the literature in your chosen field of study, and working on a literature review. Many Universities and doctoral advisors will favor a PhD dissertation that consists of 3 or more research papers that are of publishable quality. This would be a good format to pursue, as it makes it easier to then submit your papers for publication.

Table 2.1 below portrays an indicative timetable for 4-year PhD, assuming a requirement for a dissertation consisting of 3 publishable papers, plus introduction and conclusion chapters.

Table 2.1. Indicative timetable

Timeframe	Activity
Year 1	Take classes in theory and methodology. Read the literature in your chosen field, and prepare and then refine literature review. Focus your research question
Year 2	Enter the field and begin conducting your fieldwork if you are employing an inductive methodological approach. Locate or collect data set and carry out tests if you are employing a deductive methodological approach. Begin working on your first paper. Start writing your first paper
Year 3	Finish writing your first paper and write your second paper. Complete your field work if you are using inductive methods and your tests if you are using deductive methods. Refine your first and second papers
Year 4	Write your third paper, and also your introduction and the conclusion sections. Allow enough time to receive feedback from your doctoral advisor and refine your thesis accordingly. Submit your thesis at end of year 4

The doctoral process: idea, data gathering, analysis and writing, viva, and degree award

Universities have regular points of evaluation, where doctoral candidates present their progress before a committee, that will decide whether to give you the green light to continue your study. If the committee has concerns about any aspect of your thesis, or about your progress, they may give you a certain timeframe to address these concerns before they give you the green light to proceed with your study.

During this process you should be attending as many workshops, academic conferences and research seminars as you can, and engaging in as many discussions with colleagues and scholars from your own and from other institutions as you can. You should try and present your work at research seminars, conferences, and also register as a conference paper reviewer in the main conferences in your field.

Exposing your work to critical scrutiny by presenting it, is a great way to receive feedback and improve it. Getting involved as a reviewer is also a great way to learn how to evaluate research papers through practice; you gain learning that you can then apply to evaluating your own work.

Box 2.1 below offers some tips about the doctoral process from a successful PhD candidate. There are additional tips in the Appendix.

> **Box 2.1. Things I wish I knew before I started my PhD**
>
> 1. Start writing early. Don't wait for the perfect time to start writing, there is no such thing. There is however a bad time for writing and that is writing under stress, to meet a deadline. Start by taking notes, expand into chapters. There will be plenty of opportunities for revisions, writing takes practice. The more you write the better you become. Make a draft structure of your thesis and

make sure you place equal emphasis on all chapters. Make sure that you have left some time to revise your manuscript when it's done. At best, you should leave your manuscript for a few weeks before you have your final look and submit.

2. Don't wait for the 'halo moment'- do something everyday even if it looks mundane. I learned this lesson from a painter friend. He never left a day without waking up early, having his morning routine and spending 8 hours working in his studio. Not all days were equally creative, but he had to work his way to creativity. Just when I thought that a painting would take a 'halo moment' of immense creativity!

3. Do something you like, allow yourself to switch. No two days are the same, one day you might feel like reading and the other more like writing. But don't use that as the perfect excuse for procrastination. You will find millions of reasons why you are not 'ready', 'in the zone', 'read enough', etc. Do something instead of nothing. Give yourself the chance for some breaks during the year.

4. Break down the work. Take the time to think of a timeplan. Even if you don't stick to it at all times, the process of thinking a timeplan is valuable as it makes you see the forest rather than the tree. Come back to it often and revise. You will see that some parts are more difficult than others to organize – negotiating access, data collection, data analysis depending on your individual project. Make sure you allow some time for revisions and always add a week or two in your

initial thinking.

5. Do the best you can in the time that you have. That means that in the end the dissertation might not be as perfect as you thought it would be when you began the process. The good news is you will have plenty of future opportunities to rework and rethink your work in your future as a scholar. At some point, however you need to press the 'submit' button.

6. Choose your topic wisely. Strike a balance between something you like and something that is new and exciting. If no-one ever heard about your project, maybe there is a reason. One way to go about it is to read widely on a topic that you like. Reading is like a snowball process, one argument, paper, research project might take you to the next reading opportunity. Keep notes as you go along as some of your ideas might come as you go through this reading process. The better informed you are before you start the more time it will save you as you go along. That means saving you the agony of realizing that your brilliant idea is actually a very well cited paper in your field. Don't get discouraged. This is actually good news. A PhD is all about making a meaningful contribution and you just found your field.

7. Choose your supervisor wisely. Make sure you take the most out of this learning opportunity- that means: sticking to the agreed timeplan, asking questions, be prepared before your meetings and always remember this is your project and your responsibility to see it through. You are fortunate enough to have an experienced

scholar to guide you through the process.

8. Think about where you stand as a scientist. Basic assumptions about what 'truth', 'reality' and 'science' are tell a lot about one's stance as a researcher. Read before you answer. This preparation will take you a long way in your methodological choices and your future in research.

9. Allow yourself to be challenged. Take the opportunities to present your work at conferences and talk about it with friends from different fields. At some point, you need to be able to describe your project in a few sentences. If someone needs to be a fellow academic to understand what your research is all about perhaps you need to clear your thinking.

Enjoy the process! You'll come out wiser at the end and not just in terms of your academic field.

Angeliki Papachroni completed her PhD in organizational ambidexterity at the University of Warwick in 2013.

The role of the doctoral advisor

The role of the doctoral advisor is to guide you on the path to conducting research that can live up to the standard of being awarded a doctorate. The precise nature of the relationship between the student and the advisor is not a one size fits all.

It develops over time and depends on working preferences, timeframes, level of support needed, and other factors. The underlying principles however remain the same: mutual respect, trust and good will.

Your doctoral advisor will help you develop a realistic timeframe for conducting your study, help you identify and plan your methodology, will read your work and offer critical and constructive feedback, and will participate in committees that evaluate your progress annually or bi-annually, depending on the rules of your university. Your doctoral advisor will help you see the big picture when you are bogged down with the details, and will help to keep you on the path for completing your PhD.

Your advisor will also help you identify the right conferences to submit your work and to attend, and will help you develop your academic networks and links with the broader academic community. Being a successful and effective academic is a craft, and you can learn that craft during the apprenticeship period with your advisor.

Make the most of meetings with your doctoral advisor

Doctoral advisors expect PhD students to exhibit intellectual curiosity and to persevere, as the Box below illustrates.

> **Box 2.2. What I expect from my PhD students**
>
> What do I expect from my PhD students? I see the PhD as a journey of discovery to the unknown. The ability to embrace the essence of discovery which, I think, is curiosity, is needed. I always encourage my PhD students to be intellectually curious about why they see the world (and the subject they study) the way they see it and how they know that they know. This journey of (self)discovery will create the necessary space for them to reflect more effectively as they

progress through their PhD training. So a key skill for a successful PhD student, I think, is a natural curiosity to want to know, to be interested in, and to seek to understand and explain.

Related to that, I think the second key element for success is to embrace not knowing. That is the ability to show or act with extreme care and concern for understanding how things are. To do this right, however, a pre-requisite, I believe, is to admit that we really don't know all the answers. This is, perhaps, similar to a reflection of mine that each time I think I understand as much as there is to know about a subject, that is when I appreciate, inescapably, how much I do not know.

Coming to an end, the reality of being or becoming an academic refers to the ability to publish our work, something that becomes more and more challenging and complicated, especially at the top level academic journals. So perseverance is another key ingredient for success. Rejection is not a failure; it is the path to success! Keep on trying!

Dimitrios Spyridonidis is an Associate Professor of Leadership at Warwick Business School.

The role of the doctoral candidate

The responsibility for conducting and completing the doctoral research lies with you. A very important attribute is to be able to work independently. Despite the support from your advisor, you will be spending many hours working on your own. Reading, forming ideas, gathering and analyzing data, and creating drafts of chapters. A second important attribute is curiosity and a thirst for knowledge. Reading what others have done, looking out for important new research in your field, attending conferences and seminars to hear about new research. A third important capability is to be well organized. Ensure that you prepare well before meeting with your doctoral advisor, that you take notes and that you act on those notes. Ensure that you archive your research data carefully and that you are rigorous in your analysis. Ensure that you have a plan and try to keep to that plan.

A fourth important attribute is to be able to accept critique, and also be able to critique others' work. The critique will help you to improve your work. If you are not able to accept critique, then you are probably in the wrong business. A key aspect of science is that it proceeds via competition between ideas. This competition weeds out weaker ideas and enables the stronger ideas to gain currency. When others critique your work, be grateful that they took the time to read it and think about it. Take notes and consider how or whether to address these critiques, in discussion with your doctoral advisor.

You will meet many obstacles; perseverance is key to reaching your goals

The Box below offers some tips from a doctoral student who has recently completed their thesis.

> **Box 2.3. The role of the advisor and PhD candidate from a candidate's perspective**
>
> *The role of the doctoral advisor*
>
> The advisor plays an essential role in the success of a PhD thesis. He/She is the mentor for the PhD candidate, and the main force the candidate will rely on to. The influence of the advisor cannot be neglected specifically in the following areas:
>
> 1. At the very beginning, the candidate needs to choose a problematic, with the potential to be studied during several years and of growing importance. Some students have vague ideas about what they want to do and the supervisor can help to clarify and sharpen the perspective. A well-chosen dissertation topic makes a lot of difference to the success of the candidate's future career.

2. Setting regular appointments will help the candidate to advance in his/her research at a steady pace. These appointments encourage the candidate to discuss the difficulties they may encounter and set deadlines that are essential for completing various tasks.

3. Taking the time to discuss in depth the main potential contributions of the thesis is important. Because of the trust bond between the candidate and their advisor, the candidate feels more comfortable to discuss the critical issues in detail. The comments of the advisor are without doubt the main source of inspiration and are also critical to the methodological accuracy of the thesis.

4. The advisor can help the candidate integrate in the lab and the research community in general. The advisor encourages the candidate to submit their research in the leading conferences and popular events where the candidate is able to encounter other researchers in the field and to extend their network. Furthermore, it is important for the candidate to participate in conference organization and the advisor can put the candidate in touch with the organizers.

5. Giving advice to maximize publishing opportunities. The advisor has a lot of publishing experience and can give game changing advice in each and every step of the publishing process (from journal selection to submission, responding to referees, proof reading, etc.)

6. Facilitating job market integration of the candidate. Even after the defense, the PhD student still relies significantly on the help and support of the

advisor. This support can be direct by writing recommendation letters or indirect through advice and recommendations during job applications.

The role of the PhD candidate

In order to succeed in their thesis and ensure a promising career in research, PhD candidates are expected to fulfill several requirements:

1. It is essential for the candidate to be able to work independently. During the thesis period the candidate will encounter obstacles and most of the time he/she can resolve them without consulting the advisor. This period is an occasion to develop critical and independent thinking capacity.

2. Stay tuned in the major events, conferences and seminars. Although the advisor may recommend some specific events, it is the responsibility of the candidate to follow closely news about the leading conferences in the field and apply for them. Feel free to talk about such events with your fellow PhD students and lab members. Make sure you are registered in the mailing lists and you are not missing any important information.

3. Participate actively in the events of the lab and socialize with other researchers in the field. Also giving a hand in organizing such events can be a precious experience to put yourself in the organizers' shoes, and you will be more efficient next time you apply to similar events.

4. Presenting your work in different conferences and seminars is the best opportunity to have feedback on your work and also to get others familiar with your research interests and skills. This may lead in

joint projects with other researchers, and enlarge your network. It is important to work on your presentation skills.

5. Being bold enough to contact the advisor or other researchers when facing problems and dead-ends. You should not be afraid to admit to your shortcomings. The best way to overcome such problems is to talk about them. Sometimes explaining your dead-ends to another person helps you to see clearly the problem and to resolve it.

6. Not being afraid to start over. In some cases you simply need to let go. Some ideas may seem brilliant at the beginning but lose their initial interest as you get deep in the subject. As a PhD candidate you are not supposed to be perfect; even experienced researchers make poor judgments and start over.

Yeganeh Forouheshfar completed her PhD in Economics at Université Paris Dauphine PSL in 2017.

It may feel unusual and even challenging to start doctoral research, particularly if you have been working in industry before you do so. Some universities offer the degree of Doctor of Business Administration (DBA), that is more applied than a PhD, in that it has to address challenges of practice, in a theoretically informed and methodologically valid manner. Below are the insights of a student of this degree.

Box 2.4. What it feels like to be a DBA (Doctor of Business Administration) candidate

The DBA has been a transformational experience

as you need to be comfortable with uncertainty. Within the program you are operating on the cusp of academic theory and practical application. The exposure to academic literature is stimulating in that it encourages you to look at practice from different angles, examine new perspectives and experience new disciplines. The academic in the classroom is a facilitator of a developmental journey together with the other DBA participants, and with their own views being of significant value in this journey. In my experience, the challenge from the other DBA participants when presenting my ideas or perspectives has helped me develop.

Doctoral candidates need to be comfortable with this challenge and the uncertainty of not knowing all the answers. Accepting the challenge and uncertainty is part of enabling a transformational experience.

DBA participants who have been away from academia for a while will need to immerse themselves in the academic literature, and become comfortable with the different writing style to what most people experience in business. Furthermore, research methodology sessions on qualitative and quantitative methods are often needed to support DBA participants in writing their thesis. Throughout your DBA studies, you will be supported by a supervisor and DBA participants should build a strong relationship with this individual. They can act as a key critical friend to help you reflect on your learning experience and in producing your thesis.

Finally, when attempting a thesis, planning and

structure are essential. A proposed plan should be extensively discussed with your supervisor before proceeding with the thesis. I would recommend Doctoral study to curious and inquisitive minds who are looking to develop and refine their thinking at the highest level.

Oliver Walmsley is a DBA (Doctor of Business Administration) candidate at the University of Warwick.

Ethical guidelines

Doing your work within ethical boundaries is critical. Different fields have their own codes of conduct. For example, the Code of Ethics of the Academy of Management[4] has sections on general principles (responsibility, integrity, respect for people's rights and dignity), to whom the responsibilities are owed, ethical standards (on human relations, privacy and confidentiality, public statements, research and publication, and ascribing to the code of ethics).

The EU Code of Ethics on Socio-Economics Research[5] has sections on responsibilities to society, professional expertise and standards, and responsibilities to research participants. If you are uncomfortable with any aspect of your

[4] The Academy of Management Code of Ethics can be found here: https://aom.org/ethics/

[5] The EU Code of Ethics for socio-economic research can be found at
http://www.respectproject.org/ethics/412ethics.pdf

research or are facing an ethical dilemma, do not keep it to yourself. Discuss it with your doctoral advisor or with other relevant individuals and try to find a way ahead.

CHAPTER 3
METHODOLOGICAL CHOICES AND THE EXPERIMENTAL METHOD

There is a variety of methodological approaches in social science. A useful way to think about the main choices is that there are two main approaches to reasoning, deductive and inductive ones[6]. Each of these is in turn associated with certain philosophical assumptions.

Deductive approaches to reasoning involve starting from existing theory, building clear hypotheses, collecting data to test these hypotheses, and then using the results to confirm or disconfirm the hypotheses, as shown by the Figure below:

Figure 3.1. Reasoning in deductive methodological approaches

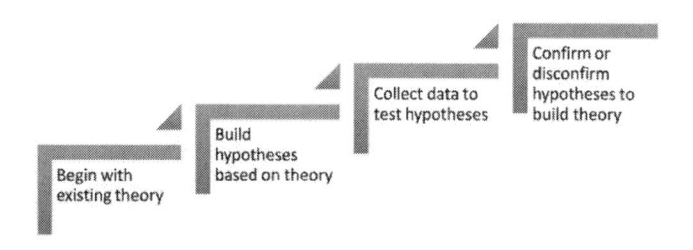

Begin with existing theory → Build hypotheses based on theory → Collect data to test hypotheses → Confirm or disconfirm hypotheses to build theory

Deductive approaches are associated with positivism; the idea that we acquire knowledge

---

[6] Bhattacherjee, A. 2012. *Social science research: Principles, methods, and practices*. Textbooks Collection. Book 3.

by experience, observation and testing, and that reality is objective, solid, and out there waiting to be discovered. Associated methodological approaches tend to be experimental and quantitative.

Inductive approaches to reasoning on the other hand, involve starting from observations (collecting data), and analyzing the data to search for emergent patterns. These patterns may be used to develop proposals, arguments or hypotheses about the processes observed, that in turn can inform theory building, as shown below:

Figure 3.2. Reasoning in inductive methodological approaches

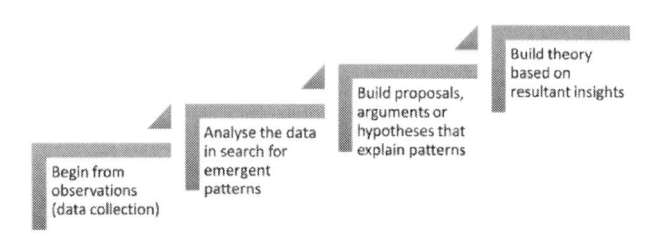

Begin from observations (data collection)

Analyse the data in search for emergent patterns

Build proposals, arguments or hypotheses that explain patterns

Build theory based on resultant insights

Inductive approaches are associated with interpretivism, the idea that we can gain knowledge via immersion in a social context, that we need to understand how the actors in a particular setting view their world, and that reality is in a continuous process of social construction. Methodological approaches tend to be ethnographic, narrative and qualitative. We expand on such approaches in chapter 4.

Because of its complexity and technical vocabulary, research methodology is often the most arduous topic that doctoral students have to grapple with. Do not give up however. This is a challenging topic for everyone. Find a methodology textbook that explains things clearly, on the recommendation of your doctoral advisor, and persevere.

Research methodology is an arduous topic;
do not give up

The experimental method

Deductive research involves the use of the experimental method to test hypotheses using a systematic protocol, in order to identify causal effects. Causal reasoning implies that A causes B, or that a variation in A causes a variation in B. Bear in mind that correlation and co-variation do not always mean that there are causal relationships in operation. Rather, proper controls need to be in operation, the results have to be replicated, and large enough data sets need to be used, to be more confident that causation is involved.

Experimental research is used in various disciplines such as sociology, psychology, physics, chemistry, biology, medicine, finance and economics. It consists of selecting experimental variables, control variables, and measuring sources of variation[7]. The experimental method uses randomization to test cause-effect relationships in a controlled

---

[7] Stock J. & Trebbi F. 2003. Who invented an instrumental variable regression? *Journal of Economic Perspectives*, 17(3): 177-194; Campbell, D. T., Stanley, J. C., & Gage, N. L. 1963. *Experimental and quasi-experimental designs for research..* Boston: Houghton Mifflin; Creswell, J. W. 2013. *Research design: Qualitative, quantitative, and mixed methods approaches.* Beverly Hills: Sage; Blakstad O., 2008. Experimental Research. Accessed at https://explorable.com/experimental-research; Baum C. F., Schaffer, M. E., & Stillman S. 2003. Instrumental variables and GMM: Estimation and testing, *Stata Journal*, 3(1): 1-31.

setting by separating causes from effects temporally. Control variables prevent the influence of external factors. Randomization is widely employed to manage issues related to endogeneity and measurement error of the explanatory equation.

There are two types of randomization. The first type is random selection, where the sample is selected randomly from a population. The second type is random assignment, where subjects are selected in a non-random manner and then randomly assigned to treatment groups. When the participants are not randomly selected or assigned, the research design is referred to as quasi-experimental.

In the experimental method, two groups of participants are considered and compared. One receives the treatment (the treatment group) and another group does not (the control group). One can then evaluate how the mean effects vary among these two groups of participants.

The "differences" method compares the difference in statistical means for the same group, before and after the treatment. The "difference-in-differences" method compares the differences in statistical means before and after the treatment, with an untreated comparison group. Box 3.1 shows an illustration of the "difference-in-differences" method used in a PhD dissertation.

Box 3.1. One example of a PhD dissertation using the experimental method

This study explores the relationship between compulsory education, educational attainment and fertility. First, it assesses how compulsory education legislation can change educational decisions. More specifically, the author use the IFLS (Indonesian Family Life Survey) database and focuses on a law implemented in 1994 in Indonesia that lengthened compulsory education from 6 to 9 years. The method used is a difference-in-differences model where the exposure of the individuals is determined by their year of birth and their region of birth.

The first source of variation is represented by individuals' year of birth. More precisely, the author distinguishes two cohorts, one being the treated cohort and the second the untreated one. Before the reform, individuals were required to stay in school until they reached 12 years of age (primary education). Since 1994, they are required to stayin school until 15 years of age. Individuals aged 16 or more in 1994 should have completed 9 years of education by 1994 and therefore should not have been impacted by the reform. These individuals represent the control group (untreated). On the contrary, individuals aged 12 or less in 1994 should have been impacted by the reform. These individuals represent the treatment group (treated).

When comparing educational attainment between the cohorts, the author does not observe a clear discontinuity before and after the reform probably because many individuals were already meeting the requirements of the reform before it was implemented. Therefore a second source of variation is considered, determining an individual's exposure to the reform: their region of birth. The reasoning is that, in regions where studying for nine years was the norm, the reform should not have a significant impact in comparison with regions where individuals were on average studying less than nine years at the time of the reform. A geographical dimension was therefore added and the intensity of the program was assumed to vary between regions of birth because of differences in initial levels of education.

The identification strategy represented by a difference-in-differences model therefore used two sources of variation: a temporal (year of birth) and a geographical variation. The author therefore tested whether children affected by the reform and born in regions that were initially lagging behind, went to school longer in comparison with children who were too old to be impacted by the reform, and with children born in other regions.

As in any empirical specification, in order to identify a causal effect, several assumptions have to be made. In the case of a difference-in-differences model, the hypothesis is that trends in the control and treatment groups should have been the same in the absence of the reform. This is known as the common trends assumption. In this study, it implies that trends in educational outcomes would have been the same in all regions. This assumption is violated if regions where the level of education was low were already catching up before the reform. Placebo tests were implemented to test for the existence of differences in trends before the reform by comparing several untreated cohorts. The author found that the law increased educational attainment more in regions where the initial level was low.

In a second stage, education is instrumented by the difference-in-differences variable to identify the causal impact of education on fertility choices (number of children and timing of pregnancies). As education and fertility are likely to be endogenous (reverse causality), it is important to use an instrumental variables model because it allows us to identify a causal impact. The results suggest that increases in education caused by the compulsory education law led to a decrease in childlessness and to a delayed first birth.

Marine de Tallancé, completed her PhD in Economics at the Université Paris-Dauphine PSL, in 2017.

How should you decide whether to use deductive or inductive methods?

The first consideration should be your research question. Certain questions can be answered more adequately by deductive, statistical, econometric methods. For example, what is the effect of a change in tax policy on savings rates? What is the effect of acquiring other companies on the market value of the buying firms? Or, what is the impact of the education public policy on poverty? In general, applied economists employ this type of methods to evaluate public policy decisions and their implementation.

Other questions can be adequately answered by inductive, qualitative methods. For example, how do organizations undertake strategic change processes, and what is the role of organizational culture in these processes? Or, how do strategists think of strategy, and do they emphasize different dimensions of strategy at different stages of institutionalizing a new strategic practice?[8]

Another consideration is your own interest and preference. Some individuals find that they feel more at home in either deductive or inductive methods. This can be influenced by past training, favorite authors or favorite teachers. A further consideration is what are the dominant methodological approaches used in the institution you would like to conduct your PhD in.

Some institutions favor predominantly deductive research, and some are welcoming to any type of approach, as long as it is carried out in a robust, valid manner. In any case, the general approach and particular methodologies within that approach will have to be discussed and agreed with your doctoral advisor. Your doctoral advisor will have their own methodological interests and preferences, that will also shape how you research your topic,

---

[8] Paroutis, S. & Heracleous, L. 2013. Discourse revisited: Dimensions and employment of first-order strategy discourse during institutional adoption. *Strategic Management Journal*, 34: 935-956.

because their expertise will be higher in these approaches.

You have some fundamental choices to make when it comes to research methods

The table below summarizes key considerations to help you decide what approach you should take.

Table 3.1. Factors in deciding on your methodological approach

Considerations	Description
Research question	Would your research question be answered more effectively with deductive or inductive approaches?
Own interest and training	Do you feel more interested in employing deductive and inductive approaches, and why? Is there training available in your chosen approach in your target institution?
Dominant approach	What is the dominant approach in the University department you would like to conduct your doctoral research in?
Doctoral advisor	Where do the methodological interests, preferences and expertise of your doctoral advisor lie?

CHAPTER 4
USING QUALITATIVE METHODS

Qualitative methods enable the researcher to go in depth and probe the meanings and interpretations that organizational and societal actors hold about particular issues. These methods are appropriate when the aim is to develop theory rather than to test specific hypotheses. This is often the case in the earlier stages of a field's development when exploratory research could be fruitful in terms of identifying key themes and building frameworks. Further, qualitative methods are appropriate when the aim is to study complex social and organizational processes where actors' own perspectives are important to uncover, such as in studies of sensemaking, negotiations, or strategy as practice. More generally, qualitative methods are useful when researchers wish to gain an in-depth understanding of a particular research context.

The research question is the primary factor for the choice of research methodology. Practical considerations are also important, such as the extent of access to a field research setting or to particular actors, and the type of data that is available (documentary, narrative, or numerical for example).

The use of qualitative methods implies certain philosophical commitments on the part of the researcher. One such commitment is interpretivism[9], the idea that accounts of social life must be faithful to the actors' own perspectives (or first-order concepts[10]); rather than simply built on second-order scientific concepts that may not bear much relation to how actors interpret their own situation.

Probing into actors' own meanings implies that actors possess and exercise a degree of agency (within certain structural constraints), rather than assuming that their choices are structurally determined. Finally, qualitative methods are accompanied by the ontological perspective that social reality is not fixed or out there waiting to be discovered, but is continually constructed via processes of social interaction and shaped by systems of meaning such as language[11].

For examples of research work on organization change that adopts these perspectives see work by Heracleous[12] and other interpretive scholars such as Andrew Pettigrew and Edgar Schein. For an extended discussion of underlying assumptions of qualitative research and how

---

[9] Burrell, G. & Morgan, G. 1979. *Sociological paradigms and organizational analysis.* Hants: Gower.

[10] Van Maanen, J. 1988. *Tales of the field: On writing ethnography.* Chicago: University of Chicago Press.

[11] Berger, P. & Luckmann, T. *The social construction of reality.* London: Penguin, 1966.

[12] Heracleous, L. 2001. An ethnographic study of culture in the context of organizational change. *Journal of Applied Behavioral Science*, 37: 426-446.

they shifted over time, see the work of Cunliffe[13].

There is a variety of qualitative methods that can be employed in social science research. Here we profile three key methods; ethnography, grounded theory and action research. For a description of the various facets of discourse analysis see Heracleous (2006, 2017)[14].

Ethnography

In qualitative empirical research, it is important to immerse oneself in the field and aim to gain insights on the research context, particularly on how actors themselves see their organizational reality. Such immersion is integral to conducting ethnography. The etymology of the term ethnography is to write about a people; the term itself refers both to the final product (the rich description of a particular people or culture), as well as the process of conducting the research.

Ethnography stems from a rich anthropological tradition. Bronislaw Malinowski was the first

---

[13] Cunliffe, A. L. 2011. Crafting qualitative research: Morgan and Smircich 30 years on. *Organizational Research Methods*, 14: 647-673.

[14] Heracleous, L. 2006. *Discourse, interpretation, organization*. Cambridge: Cambridge University Press; Heracleous, L. 2017. Discourse theory. In Langley, A. & Tsoukas, H. (Eds.), *The Sage Handbook of Process Organization Studies*, Beverly Hills, Sage: 190-203.

anthropologist to introduce the concept of participant observation (to observe a group while participating in their activities). He was born in 1884 in what is now Poland and conduced his anthropological work in Papua New Guinea and the Trobriand islands. When the first world war broke out he was in Papua, and the Australian authorities offered him two choices; to go to prison until the end of the war (as an Austrian/Hungarian), or to be exiled to the Trobriand islands. He chose the latter, and at first actively avoided the natives, who were at the time considered "savages". In time he became lonely and decided to participate in their society, where he formed close friendships and was even rumoured to have fallen in love. He was the first anthropologist to bring anthropology "off the verandah", beyond structured interviews, to include participant observation that aimed to grasp the native's point of view.

Arthur Reginald Radcliffe-Brown was born in 1881 in Birmingham and studied at Trinity College Cambridge. He conducted his ethnographic studies at the Andaman Islands (Bay of Bengal) and also in Western Australia. He later became professor at the Universities of Chicago and Oxford. He is the originator of the intellectual perspective of functionalism, that aims to explain how practices, norms and institutions work together to sustain social stability, and explains the existence of these practices in terms of their social function. Malinowski was also a functionalist but in another sense, suggesting that social practices exist because they satisfy basic biological needs.

Claude Levi-Strauss was born in 1908 in Belgium and educated at the Sorbonne in Paris. He then started teaching at the University of Sao Paolo in Brazil, where he initiated his first expeditions to study indigenous tribes in the Amazon rainforest. Subsequently he moved to the United States where he published his first anthropological works on structures of myth, kinship and food preparation. He is one of the originators of the intellectual perspective of structuralism, the idea is that social practices are interconnected in systematic forms that give rise to meanings, in the same way that the rules of grammar structure language-in-use. More recent noted anthropologists include Clifford Geertz[15] in symbolic anthropology and John van Maanen[16] in the organization studies fields.

In order to conduct ethnography, you will need to identify an appropriate organization or setting, and negotiate access; decide whether to conduct overt or covert research (the ethical issue of informed consent by participants must be considered here), decide whether to conduct

---

[15] Geertz, C. 1973. *The interpretation of cultures.* New York: Basic Books.

[16] Van Maanen, J. 1988. *Tales of the field: On writing ethnography.* Chicago: University of Chicago Press.

participant or non-participant observation, and read more about the various roles that the ethnographer can fulfil (clinician, apprentice or confidante for example). Ethnographic research can be emotionally demanding, especially in unusual contexts[17].

Once you start the research, you must take initiative to develop links and networks of actors that can act as informants, and conduct theoretical sampling of people and events for deeper study. It is important to be meticulous in recording field notes in various modes, and to archive and manage the data carefully. This will make the process more manageable and effective when you start to analyze the data, and will minimize the risk that you forget or omit to record important observations.

Ethnographers start to analyze the data as early as possible, moving from first-order concepts as used by actors to second-order concepts of social science in order to build more broadly applicable frameworks. Data analysis can employ sensitizing frameworks, grounded theory or tools of discourse analysis, and is characterized by the hermeneutic circle of iteratively going from data to theory and vice versa, until saturation of understanding is reached.

---

[17] De Rond, M. 2012. Soldier, surgeon, photographer, fly: Fieldwork beyond the comfort zone. *Strategic Organization*, 10; 156-262.

Validity of analysis can be improved via a number of ways, such as contextual understanding of observed actions and practices, respondent validation, triangulation of data, method and theory, researcher reflexivity (reflecting and making explicit one's own role, values and biases), prolonged immersion in the field and rich description, and trustworthiness and credibility of the account.

Challenges of conducting ethnography include the risk of going native (becoming enculturated and losing the critical distance needed); managing to keep "second order" renditions close to actors' "first-order" interpretations; distinguishing between "operational data" or data that is unaffected by your presence as researcher, versus "representational data"[18] that is affected (even though both types can be valuable); being misled by informants; and dealing effectively with large volumes of data.

Grounded theory

Grounded theory is a methodological approach that involves building theory that emerges from, and is intimately linked with, systematically collected and closely analyzed data[19]. Grounded

---

[18] Van Maanen, J. 1979. The fact of fiction in organizational ethnography. *Administrative Science Quarterly*, 24: 539-550.

[19] Glazer, B. G. & Strauss, A. L. 1967. *The discovery of grounded theory.* Chicago: Aldine. Strauss, A. L. & Corbin, J. 1994. Grounded theory methodology: An overview. In *Handbook of Qualitative Research*, NK Denzin and YS

theory evolves through an interplay between analysis and data collection, via the constant comparative method of comparing newly collected data with existing data, and iterating between data and emergent theory. Once the theory begins to emerge, this process enables ongoing exploration and verification of relationships among concepts that comprise the theory.

The analytical process begins with open coding, where the main themes related to the phenomenon of interest emerge. This is followed by axial coding, where relationships between the emergent themes are explored and identified. Finally, there is selective coding, where themes of special interest for emergent theory are explored further and more intentionally in the data corpus. Coding is an ongoing, iterative process between data, the development of the codes, and emergent theory. A move to subsequent stages occurs when the researcher believes that further data and analysis in an existing stage will not contribute additional insights.

The outcome of grounded theory approaches can be represented in coding trees, such as the one found for example in Heracleous et al.'s study of the reasons for which Xerox failed to commercialize most of the groundbreaking

---

Lincoln, CA: Sage: 273-285.

inventions that arose from its research facility, Xerox PARC[20]. Through coding analysis of a variety of documents and other narrative sources, the authors identified 15 first-order concepts, that coalesced into 7 second-order categories, and then into 3 aggregate concepts that linked with emergent theory. The 3 aggregate concepts that explained why Xerox was unable to commercialize PARC's inventions were "dominant logic", "disjointed inventions" and "organizational tensions".

Grounded theory requires a delicate balancing act that involves possessing theoretical awareness that sensitizes the researcher to certain relationships, but also allowing the data to speak for itself. It also requires the ability to be reflexive about the researcher's own perspective and it necessitates the ability to understand the research context and to read between the lines of first order concepts based on this understanding. Grounded theory, like ethnography, is time consuming and the researcher has to deal with a high volume of data. A useful discussion of the application and challenges of using of grounded theory in doctoral studies can be found in Fendt and Sachs (2008)[21].

---

[20] Heracleous, L., Papachroni, A., Andriopoulos, C. & Gotsi, M. 2017. Structural ambidexterity and competency traps: Insights from Xerox PARC. *Technological Forecasting and Social Change*, 117: 327-338.

[21] Fendt, J. & Sachs, W. 2008. Grounded theory method in

Let the data speak to you when employing grounded theory

management research. *Organizational Research Methods*, 11: 430-455.

Action research

The originator of action research is the social scientist Kurt Lewin, born in 1890 in Poland, who described it as "comparative research on the conditions and effects of various forms of social action and research leading to social action"[22]. Some well-known tools and concepts that derive from action research include force-field analysis[23] defensive routines, espoused theories and theories-in-use[24], process consultation and career anchors[25].

Essentially action research is a process of gathering research data in the process of helping organizations deal with challenges they face. The ultimate research objective is to derive from the intervention broader principles or actionable knowledge that can help other organizations dealing with similar challenges or that can shed light on a phenomenon of interest. A detailed example of an action research intervention that resulted in theoretical insights can be found in Heracleous and Marshak (2004)[26].

---

[22] Lewin, K. 1946. Action research and minority problems. *Journal of Social Issues*, 2: 34-46.

[23] Lewin, K. 1951. *Field theory in social science*. New York: Harper.

[24] Argyris, C. 1995. Action science and organizational learning. *Journal of Managerial Psychology*, 10(5): 20-26.

[25] Schein, E. H. 1995. Process consultation, action research and clinical inquiry: are they the same? *Journal of Managerial Psychology*, 10(6): 14-19.

Action research therefore combines both action (helping organizations with actual challenges) as well as research (contributing to knowledge). It is usually (but not always) initiated by the client; it involves opportunistic elements, in that the actions to be taken, data collection, and potential theoretical insights cannot be specified in advance and can be pursued according to how the action research process develops. Most of the data are gathered in real time and it can involve both participant and non-participant observation and other sources such as interviews and document analysis. The researcher is seen by the client organization as a consultant or expert, and therefore it is important to have credibility in that regard. The more the researcher is seen as helpful, the more the organizational participants will allow the researcher to go behind the scenes and learn more about the organization.

One challenge with using qualitative methods is that, because of their inductive, emergent nature, you will gather a large amount of unstructured, rich data, where it may initially not be clear what insights are emerging. Take notes, go back and forth between your interpretations and the data, and patterns will begin to emerge.

---

[26] Heracleous, L. & Marshak, R. J. 2004. Conceptualizing organizational discourse as situated symbolic action. *Human Relations*, 57: 1285-1312.

Look for emergent patterns when using qualitative methods

The action research process often involves joint diagnosis of the client issues, action planning, action taking, evaluating the consequences of initiatives, and specifying the learning[27]. Some key decisions that the researcher has to make

---

[27] Susman, G. I. & Evered, R. D. 1979. An assessment of the scientific merits of action research. *Administrative Science Quarterly*, 23: 582-603.

include how overt the research aspect of the intervention should be, how visible the data collection methods should be, and how risky the design of the action research intervention can be[28]. The Table below summarizes the three qualitative methods discussed in this chapter and when they might be employed. The circumstances described are not absolute or mutually exclusive, but they give an idea of when a method may be suitable.

Table 4.1. Qualitative research methods and their use

Research method	Nature of method	When method could be used
Ethnography	The in-depth study of societal or organizational cultures through immersion by the researcher in that context. Researcher may be a participant or non-participant observer and aims to	When the research question requires deep understanding of the context; when extensive access to the organization makes this approach feasible; when there is sufficient time

---

[28] Huxham, C. & Vangen, S. Researching organizational practice through action research:

Case studies and design choices. *Organizational Research Methods*, 2003, *6*, 383–403.

	understand the social world of participants from their own points of view	available to immerse oneself in the setting
Grounded theory	The development of theoretical constructs and frameworks in an inductive, iterative manner, through constant comparison between data and emergent theory. Coding proceeds from open, to axial, to selective coding and is often represented in coding trees. Researcher needs to balance emergence of concepts from data analysis, with awareness of existing theory	At an early stage of a field, when existing theories may not take account of important influencing factors; when data gathered point towards insights not captured by existing theory and call for deeper exploration; when inductive approach is needed but there is not sufficient time to conduct an ethnography

Action research	The process of assisting a social group in their challenges, while at the same time gathering data for research purposes. It is often initiated by the client and involves joint diagnosis of issues, action planning, action taking, evaluating the consequences of initiatives, and specifying the learning	When client organization faces challenges that researcher can assist with and invites researcher to do so; when client agrees that data from interventions may be used for research purposes; when outcomes may be discerned and linked to interventions

As is apparent from the discussion in this chapter, many aspects of qualitative methods are not mutually exclusive, and these methods are in fact interconnected. For example, reflexivity is important in all qualitative methods. Grounded theory can be used to analyze ethnographic data, and participant observation can be used in ethnography as well as action research.

From a research methods perspective it is important to have an approach that is appropriate for addressing the research question; to gather sufficient amount of data, of the right type; to conduct a robust and defensible analysis; to theorize in a way that is supported by the analysis; and to write the research up in a clear, transparent and trustworthy manner.

CHAPTER 5
MAKING A THEORETICAL CONTRIBUTION

Making a theoretical contribution is a pre-requisite for getting a PhD, and for publishing your research in a high quality journal. The first step to being able to make a theoretical contribution is to identify a research gap. Identifying a gap and working to address it is an ongoing process as your research develops. As you improve your knowledge of the available literature, and explore under the guidance of your doctoral advisor, research gaps become apparent. Some examples of a research gap, and therefore opportunities to make a theoretical contribution, are below.

Research gaps and potential for making contributions

1. Where empirical research does not support the predictions of a theory. For example, agency theory is the dominant theory in corporate governance, and addresses the so-called agency problem; that managers and directors are agents of shareholders who should be properly monitored so they do not engage in opportunistic behavior. Agency theory offers a number of prescriptions to improve governance. For example, that the roles of corporate CEO and Chair of the board should be held by two different individuals rather than a single person; and

that there should be a significant external, independent director presence on board of directors (in relation to internal, executive directors). Yet, a number of studies and meta-analyses have shown that these prescriptions have no consistent correlation with company performance[29]. One opportunity to make a contribution here is to explain why the theory's predictions do not stand up empirically, identify boundary conditions where they would do so, or offer an improved version of the theory where prescriptions can be supported empirically.

2. A research gap exists where there are alternative, mutually inconsistent explanations of the same phenomenon. For example, the key concern of strategic management research is to identify what leads to higher firm performance. The industrial organization paradigm and the resource based view offer different, competing explanations[30]. Industrial organization proposes that outperformance is based on industry characteristics, and suggests that a firm can select particular market niches where returns can be higher,

---

[29] Dalton, D. R., Hitt, M. A., Certo, S. T., Dalton, C. M. 2007. The fundamental agency problem and its mitigation. *Academy of Management Annals*, 1: 1-64.

[30] Heracleous, L. 2003. *Strategy and organization: Realizing strategic management.* Cambridge: Cambridge University Press.

and compete in these niches. The resource based view suggests that outperformance results from internal core competencies that a firm invests in and develops over time; that are valuable, rare, inimitable and non-substitutable[31]. Research that disaggregated sources of performance between external and internal factors has made a significant contribution to our understanding of strategic management and sources of outperformance[32].

---

[31] Barney, J., Write, M. & Ketchen, D. J. 2001. The resource-based view of the firm: Ten years after 1991. *Journal of Management*, 27: 625-641.

[32] McGahan, A. M. & Porter, M. E. 1997. How much does industry matter, really? *Strategic Management Journal*, 18: 15-30; Bowman, E. H. & Helfat, C. E. 2001. Does corporate strategy matter? *Strategic Management Journal*, 22: 1-23.

Inconsistent explanations for the same phenomenon present an opportunity for contribution

3. A research gap exists where there is low codification of methodologies, perhaps because they are novel or because they are being transferred from a different field. For example, in the 1990s organization discourse emerged as an important method for conducting interpretive studies of organizations through analysis of textual materials such as documents, naturally occurring conversations, or interviews[33]. Discourse analysis was already established in

---

[33] Heracleous, L. 2006. *Discourse, interpretation, organization*. Cambridge: Cambridge University Press.

linguistics and sociology, but at the time was a novel approach in organization theory. The large number of theories and intellectual approaches (for example hermeneutics, rhetoric, metaphor, conversation analysis) that such an analysis could draw from have afforded significant opportunities to make a contribution by adapting these methods for organizational analysis and addressing new or established themes in organization theory (for example organization change, organization culture, legitimacy or identity)[34]. Currently, emergent visual and video methods in strategic management and organization theory are offering a similar opportunity to make methodological contributions[35].

4. A research gap exists when there is a sense of stagnation or incrementalism in a field, and there are calls for new perspectives or re-direction of inquiry. This occurred for example at different stages of the leadership

---

[34] Heracleous, L. and Barrett, M. 2001. Organizational change as discourse: Communicative actions and deep structures in the context of IT Implementation. *Academy of Management Journal*, 44: 755-778; Barrett, M., Heracleous, L., & Walsham, G. 2013. A rhetorical approach to IT diffusion: Reconceptualizing the ideology-framing relationship in computerization movements. *MIS Quarterly*, 37: 201-220.

[35] Knight, E., Paroutis, S. & Heracleous, L. 2018. The power of powerpoint: A visual perspective on meaning making in strategy. Forthcoming, *Strategic Management Journal*

field, that went through periods of dominance of trait analysis, the leadership styles approach, contingency theory, and charismatic and transformational leadership. At each stage there was a sense that something new was needed, when additional studies delivered small, incremental rather than significant new understanding. This sense of stagnation gave birth to new approaches. Another example is the strategy field; the emergence of the strategy as practice perspective in the late 1990s[36] for example is a result of dissatisfaction with paucity of understanding existing approaches offered about how strategy is actually carried out; that is, what do strategists do, how they develop strategy, how they talk about it, and what strategy means to them[37].

5. Research gaps and opportunities for contribution also exist when a field is at an embryonic or early stage, or when there is increased interest in it. For example, the field of organizational ambidexterity (the

---

[36] Whittington, R. 1996. Strategy as practice. *Long Range Planning*, 29: 731-735.

[37] Paroutis, S. & Heracleous, L. 2013. Discourse revisited: Dimensions and employment of first-order strategy discourse during institutional adoption. *Strategic Management Journal*, 34: 935-956; Knight, E., Paroutis, S. & Heracleous, L. 2018. The power of powerpoint: A visual perspective on meaning making in strategy. Forthcoming, *Strategic Management Journal*.

ability of a firm to balance exploration of new avenues for growth and innovation, with exploitation of current resources and offerings) is at a growth stage and there are areas where contributions are needed. Ambidexterity theory suggests that firms can create separate subsidiaries to innovate and then incorporate the innovations in their traditional business; or that individuals can learn to make their own decisions on how to balance competing demands; or that the organization can go through intermittent periods of high exploration or high exploitation through a punctuated equilibrium pattern. However, in practice, it is unclear how to implement some of these prescriptions, and they often fail, such as in the well-known Xerox PARC case[38]. Understanding how ambidexterity is implemented[39], and the reasons for failure offers the opportunity for a contribution. Another opportunity for contribution in this field is that we do not know enough about how individuals deal with ambidexterity

---

[38] Heracleous, L., Papachroni, A., Andriopoulos, C. & Gotsi, M. 2017. Structural ambidexterity and competency traps: Insights from Xerox PARC. *Technological Forecasting and Social Change,* 117: 327-338.

[39] Heracleous, L. & Wirtz, J. 2014. Sustainable competitive advantage at Singapore Airlines: Dual strategy as mastering paradox. *Journal of Applied Behavioral Science,* 50: 150-170; Heracleous, L. 2013. Quantum strategy at Apple Inc. *Organizational Dynamics,* 42: 92-99.

tensions, since most ambidexterity studies have been carried out at the organizational level, so a study addressing the individual level could make a contribution[40].

Box 5.1 below offers a summary of the above discussion.

Box 5.1. A research gap, and an opportunity for making a contribution, exists when:

1. Empirical research does not support the predictions of theory

2. There are alternative, mutually inconsistent explanations of the same phenomenon

3. There is low codification of methodologies

4. A sense of stagnation of incrementalism in a field

5. When a field is at an early or embryonic stage

---

[40] Papachroni, A., Heracleous, L. & Paroutis, S. 2016. In pursuit of ambidexterity: Managerial reactions to innovation-efficiency tensions. *Human Relations*, 69: 1791-1822.

Building a theory is an incremental, relational and also precarious process

Additional opportunities for theoretical contributions

In some cases there may not be an explicit research gap, but a theoretical contribution could still be made, as follows:

1. By employing a new lens to conceptualize a phenomenon, that affords insights not offered by existing approaches. This could be done by importing a theory from a different field into organization theory or management for example. Examples could be viewing organization change as discourse,[41] examining information technology diffusion

---

[41] Heracleous, L. and Barrett, M. 2001. Organizational change as discourse: Communicative actions and deep structures in the context of IT Implementation. *Academy of Management Journal*, 44: 755-778.

through rhetorical analysis[42] or using legal theory to inform aspects of agency theory.[43]

2. Continuing on the above approach, a contribution could be made by challenging a dominant perspective and offering credible alternatives. One example is the challenge of the tenets of agency theory through legal theory. Legal theory re-defines the principal in the agency relationship (the company rather than the shareholders); redefines the status of the board (as autonomous fiduciaries rather than shareholders' agents) and recasts the role of directors (as mediating hierarchs rather than monitors)[44]. Such contributions can be "revelatory" rather than "incremental"[45] because they offer insight beyond "normal science" or dominant, accepted lens for viewing a topic.

---

[42] Barrett, M., Heracleous, L., & Walsham, G. 2013. A rhetorical approach to IT diffusion: Reconceptualizing the ideology-framing relationship in computerization movements. *MIS Quarterly*, 37: 201-220.

[43] Lan, L. L. & Heracleous, L. 2010. Rethinking agency theory: The view from law. *Academy of Management Review*, 35: 294-314.

[44] Lan, L. L. & Heracleous, L. 2010. Rethinking agency theory: The view from law. *Academy of Management Review*, 35: 294-314; Heracleous, L. & Lan, L. L. 2012. Agency theory, institutional sensitivity, and inductive reasoning: Towards a legal perspective. *Journal of Management Studies*, 49: 223-239.

[45] Corley K. G. & Gioia, D. A. 2011. Building theory about theory building. What constitutes a theoretical contribution? *Academy of Management Review*, 36: 12-32.

3. Bringing different theoretical lenses together with empirical data can facilitate the making of a theoretical contribution because it encourages new perspectives on an issue. An example is a study that combined empirical data from interviews of practicing strategists on what strategy means to them, together with discourse theory, institutional theory and practice theory. This study uncovered four dimensions of how strategists viewed strategy (functional, contextual, identity and metaphorical); and theorized how these dimensions were employed by strategists in the process of institutionalization of a strategy function[46].

4. Finally, one way to extend the impact of a research program is to make applied contributions. You can think in terms of practitioner relevance, and prepare manuscripts that clarify how the research can address particular challenges that practitioners face. In this way, in addition to "scientifically useful," research can be "practically useful."[47]

---

[46] Paroutis, S. & Heracleous, L. 2013. Discourse revisited: Dimensions and employment of first-order strategy discourse during institutional adoption. *Strategic Management Journal*, 34: 935-956.

[47] Corley K. G. & Gioia, D. A. 2011. Building theory about theory building. What constitutes a theoretical contribution? *Academy of Management Review*, 36: 12-32.

Box 5.2. A theoretical contribution may also be made by:

1. Employing a new lens to conceptualize a phenomenon that affords novel insights

2. Challenging a dominant perspective and offering credible alternatives

3. Bringing different theoretical lenses together with empirical data

4. Engaging with and helping to address practical challenges is an applied contribution

Hard work and persistence are essential to making a theoretical contribution

From the perspective of a doctoral candidate, the requirement of making a theoretical contribution can be daunting. There are several practices that may help however, some of which we discussed in chapter 2 on the process of conducting a PhD. These include exposing your work to critical scrutiny, being involved in reviewing for conferences, reading journal papers with a critical eye, and discussing with your doctoral advisor whether your emergent findings can lead a contribution or not, and why. Below are some insights from a PhD candidate on making a meaningful contribution.

> **Box 5.3. Making a meaningful contribution – 10 things I wish I knew before I started my PhD**
>
> My University's requirements for the Award of a research degree read as follows: "To satisfy the requirements for the degree of PhD, a thesis shall constitute a substantial original contribution to knowledge which is, in principle, worthy of peer-reviewed publication". Pretty scary stuff, huh? Well, actually not! Here are 10 tactics towards coming up with an original idea and making a meaningful contribution – in my mind, the hardest part of the PhD.
>
> 1. Write mini-papers. Put your initial ideas on paper by writing approximately 4000 words in line with the structure of a peer-reviewed publication. This will force you to clearly state the literature gap, describe and explain your findings as well as your contribution beyond abstract terms. The reflective process that goes along with it gives you

and your supervisors the chance to evaluate the potential of your ideas early on and to improve them before you invest too much time, e.g. in a full-fledged literature review.

2. Use Special Issues of Journals for inspiration. Sometimes you may feel overwhelmed by your data and you may see too many interesting ways for framing your research. If this is the case, look at the top-rated journals in your area and find out what submissions for Special Issues they currently invite; maybe one fits with your research interest and/or data. If this is the case, use the call to focus your framing, analysis, and contribution. If you make it time-wise you can even consider a submission.

3. Serve as a reviewer. By reviewing others' work e.g. for conferences, you may draw connections you were previously unaware of, get to know of a stream of literature outside of your regular field of study that you can draw from, or become familiar with a novel method, which may enable you to tease out additional findings from your data. Additionally, this exercise sharpens your eye for a good contribution – a useful skill for one's own writing.

4. Participate in a research community. Research communities usually form around topics, phenomena, or theories and provide multiple opportunities for networking and voluntarism. Besides that they also keep you informed about cutting-edge thinking in their domain, grant exclusive or early-bird access to resources and may even present you with opportunities for

friendly reviews. All of the above comprise useful sources for input and feedback on your evolving ideas towards a strong contribution.

5. Revisit practice to fuel theory. Oftentimes PhD candidates argue in their thesis to address an "under-researched area". Albeit a perfectly acceptable justification for choosing a topic, it is a risky strategy. Very few issues with such a claim would withstand an examiner duly scrutinizing your work. Consequently try to construct an interesting and relevant puzzle worth further research instead. An effective way for doing so is to look at the actual practice of your research area. Normally, this enables you very quickly to uncover relevant challenges and unsolved problems.

6. Let the data speak to you. Especially when applying inductive reasoning you do not know right from the start what to expect from your data and therefore cannot clearly anticipate your contribution up front. This is a nerve-racking process — agreed. However, on the upside it provides you with the opportunity to simply be interested in a phenomenon or topic without already having the full storyline in mind. By being open-minded about the findings, you increase your chances of a strong contribution because your thinking is not tightly coupled and thereby limited by previous work.

7. Examine your data from different points of view. As with many things in life, obvious things are seldom worthwhile things. The same goes for contributions. They require you to go beyond

scratching the evident surface but to combine, split, drill down, zoom out, and iterate your data in various different ways. Allow time for these analysis steps and prepare several scenarios of data sub-sets on a short-list that you can then effectively discuss with your supervisors before settling on the final topic and your contribution.

8. Focus! Focus! Focus! Don't try to do too much. This goes for your overall thesis as well as for any paper that you publish based on it. By throwing together too many concepts and by drawing on too many literatures you reduce the credibility and effectiveness of your work. Of course, this is easier said than done. However, by continuously revising your text and by forcing yourself to state a manageable number of contributions in a simple and crisp way, you usually achieve clarity on what you try to do for yourself, your readers and ultimately the examiners of your PhD thesis.

9. Do not re-invent the wheel. The sheer number of different disciplines, theories, methodologies, and agendas that has developed over time in social and natural sciences constitutes a big challenge, especially for scholars new to the game such as PhD candidates. For this reason, it is important to keep one's eyes open to alternative conceptualizations and terms. When in doubt ask your supervisor, colleagues, or your research community. By knowing the right words to key in databases, the danger of re-inventing the wheel is mitigated and the chances for making an original contribution increased.

10. Be realistic and modest. When deciding on the

topic of your PhD research and your likely contribution, make sure that you take time, money, and resource constraints into account. They may directly influence what can realistically be achieved and what cannot. In addition, keep in mind that the chances that you will become the next Michael Porter in management studies or the next Albert Einstein in physics may be slim (sorry to disappoint). Consequently adopt a modest approach to framing your contribution and be positively surprised, if your work is appraised as even more relevant as you originally thought. This will mitigate opposition of your thesis examiners and of journal reviewers.

The above shows that making a contribution worthy of a PhD degree is no magic. Hard work, determination, and hopefully the above recommendations, will set you up for success. That means: Put away your coffee and start now - no excuses!

Christina Wawarta is in the process of completing her PhD on strategy tools in practice in 2019 at the Warwick Business School.

It is useful to have an idea whether the aim of your intended contribution is for theory generation, theory elaboration, or theory testing. It is possible to make a contribution along more than one of these interrelated domains. Theory generation is more likely to be published in a high end journal than the other two, because it is regarded as more revelatory rather than incremental.

A theoretical contribution involves a balancing act; a contribution should be focused enough to be precise, but also broad enough to matter. A theoretical argument that is too narrowly focused runs the risk of becoming esoteric, accessible to just a few specialists, or even trivial. A theoretical argument that is too broad does not go deep enough to be a solid contribution.

It is useful to remember what theory is, and make sure that a theory is indeed being proposed. A theory is a statement of the interrelationships between a number of key concepts, that is intended to shed light on a challenge, a situation or an outcome. In order to clarify that a theory is indeed being proposed, that could be novel enough to constitute a contribution, one could ensure that it answers the following questions: (1) what factors or variables are involved? (2) how are these factors related? (3) why are these factors relevant, and what is the logic of their particular interrelationships? (4) what are the limitations or boundary conditions of the theory proposed? In other words, who, where and when does the theory apply (or does not apply)[48]?

[48] Whetten, D. A. 1989. What constitutes a theoretical contribution? *Academy of Management Review*, 14: 490–495.

In order to develop your expertise in identifying research gaps and proposing theoretical contributions, it is good practice to read published papers from high quality journals and try to work out the answer to these questions for yourself. With practice, identifying and evaluating a contribution will become easier.

CHAPTER 6
PUBLISHING YOUR WORK

If you are doing a PhD because you would like to have an academic career as opposed to working in industry, it is imperative for the success of your career that you can publish academic articles in high quality journals. Universities' reputations are based primarily on research productivity and impact. Quality of teaching, student experience and other factors are of course important, but these alone do not create world class universities. Further, highly ranked Universities will promote academics up the academic ladder mainly based on their publications; provided other factors such as their teaching, collegiality or administrative contributions are up to scratch.

If you write your PhD using the structure of three or four research papers (as opposed to one long narrative), then you will be one step closer to being ready to submit papers to academic journals. Submissions can start as soon as possible during your study, and continue in earnest after the successful defense of your thesis. Given the limited tenure clock period for most academics (six or seven years), submitting and publishing papers as soon as possible is essential.

A journal paper, much like a PhD thesis, typically has to make a theoretical contribution to be accepted for publication. Making a theoretical contribution is an issue that you will have considered while planning and conducting your research. However, it comes into stark relief when you submit an academic paper, because journal submissions at high quality journals are under detailed scrutiny, at a more intense level than any other kind of publication. This is the so-called double-blind peer review system. The author does not know who the reviewers are, and the reviewers do not know who the authors are. That is, at least in theory; if you present your work at conferences and then submit it to a journal, for example, it is possible that if the reviewers are aware of your presentation, they could guess your identity.

Why papers may be rejected

High quality journals typically accept between 5 to 8% of submitted papers, after at least two rounds of revisions, so it is reasonable to expect rejection at different parts of the lengthy review process. There are many reasons a paper may be rejected. Some papers are desk-rejected by the editor (they are not sent out for review) for many reasons including: because their theme may not fit what the journal is interested in or publishes, because the writing or presentation are sloppy, or because they are deemed of such low quality that they would not stand a chance in the review process[49].

Once a paper is sent to reviewers for peer review, a key reason it may get rejected is that the reviewers do not think it makes a novel or substantial enough theoretical contribution. They may believe that it makes an incremental contribution, whereas the journal it is submitted to may tend to only publish papers that make a substantial or revelatory contribution[50].

Another key reason for rejection is methodological; that is, the methodology may be unclear, inappropriate, or not well executed. The conclusions or findings may not be well supported by the evidence or by the arguments made. The logic or veracity of the arguments may be weak. Or, scholars who work in a different paradigm and may be unfamiliar with or disagree with the approach taken in the paper, may be asked to review it.

Finally, a paper may be rejected if when asked to revise and resubmit, the authors do not take enough care and attention in responding to reviewers' concerns, both in the text as well as in the response document to the editor and reviewers. Reviewers may spend several hours conducting a manuscript review, and if they feel that the authors did not take their concerns

---

[49] Kilduff, M. 2007. Editor's comments: The top ten reasons your paper might not be sent out for review. *Academy of Management Review*, 32: 700-702.

[50] Corley K. G. & Gioia, D. A. 2011. Building theory about theory building. What constitutes a theoretical contribution? *Academy of Management Review*, 36: 12-32.

seriously in the revised manuscript, they are likely to recommend rejection.

It is clear therefore that a paper may be rejected for a variety of factors[51]. This is part of the scientific process, that is Darwinian in nature. Weaker papers get weeded out, and the ones that survive the demanding review process are seen as more valid and trustworthy. Even seasoned scholars have their papers regularly rejected, which is one indication of the robustness of the review process.

---

[51] Daft, R. L. 1985. Why I recommended that your manuscript be rejected and what you can do about it. In *Publishing in the Organizational Sciences*, L. L. Cummings & P. J. Frost (Eds.), Homewood, IL: Irwin, 193-209; Patriotta, G. 2017. Crafting papers for publication: Novelty and convention in academic writing. *Journal of Management Studies*, 54: 747-759.

Rejection by journals is to be expected, do not take it personally

Before you submit your paper

Before you submit your paper, ask your colleagues or research collaborators who are not co-authors for journal-style reviews of your work; and offer the same in return. Friendly reviews can help you push the paper at a higher level of quality that it stands a chance in the vigorous review process of high quality journals. Also, take the chance to present your work to critical audiences such as through submissions to high quality conferences and delivering seminars to good Universities.

Further, you can try to be your own worst critic. It is difficult to be critical with our own work, but if we can let it sit for a few weeks and come back to it, it is surprising how we can often see it with different eyes and see shortcomings that were not apparent before. It is important to expose our work to critical scrutiny because research shows that we tend to overestimate the quality of our own manuscripts in relation to others' manuscripts; and we tend to have the highest levels of agreement with editorial decisions that are favorable to our own manuscripts and unfavorable to others' manuscripts[52]. Exposing your work to critique prior to journal submission, makes it more likely to withstand the demanding journal review process.

Learning how to review academic papers is a craft, as is learning to write papers. Volunteer to review papers submitted to the main conferences in your field. Gradually you can work yourself up to reviewing journal papers. When you see papers from a reviewer's perspective, you also improve your own writing process.

An often underestimated issue is the quality of writing. Make sure you write clearly and in a

---

[52] Van Lange, P. A. M. 1999. Why authors believe that reviewers stress limiting aspects of manuscripts: The SLAM effect in peer review. *Journal of Applied Social Psychology*, 29: 2550-2566.

structured way[53]. Journal reviewers can get annoyed with sloppy writing and that could be a reason your paper is rejected. Friendly reviewers should be able to point out if the manuscript is clear or if it is convoluted. Below are some writing tips from a PhD student who recently completed his dissertation.

> **Box 6.1. Starting the craft of writing**
>
> It was only into the second year of my PhD that I started to appreciate the craft of writing. I knew that writing was hard. It was a relief, however, when I attended a writing workshop at an academic conference, to find out from senior academics that writing is not a gift but a skill that requires constant practice[54].
>
> Three tips have helped my productive writing, namely: write more often and more regularly; continuously improve writing style; and, converse clearly and coherently with the audience from beginning to the end. Firstly, I have learnt to prioritize writing time in my diary—so that I develop a routine and maintain the habit[55]. Secondly, in practicing the skill of writing this involves not only rewriting but also

---

[53] Ragins, B. R. 2012. Editor's comments: Reflections on the craft of clear writing. *Academy of Management Review*, 37: 493-501.

[54] Ragins, B. R. 2012. Editor's comments: Reflections on the craft of clear writing. *Academy of Management Review*, 37: 493–501.

[55] Silvia, P. J. 2007. *How to Write a Lot: A Practical Guide to Productive Academic Writing.*

making multiple iterations to revised work—that address matters of content, organization and tone[56]. Thirdly, in communicating with the audience, I am glad to hear from my supervisors, proofreaders and conference reviewers about suggestions that improve the clarity, parsimony and interest of my argumentation, discourse or narrative[57].

If I can make one suggestion to prospective PhD candidates, it is to attend a craft of writing workshop as early as possible—and enjoy reading the available resources.

Orlando J. Fernandes completed his PhD in corporate governance at the University of Warwick in 2017.

The paper revision process

If a paper is given a "revise and resubmit" decision, no matter how disheartening or critical the feedback from the reviewers, don't take it personally and don't lose heart or patience. Persistence is key. A paper may be rejected by 2

---

[56] Strunk, W., & White, E. B. 2013. *Elements of Style* (4th ed.). Essex, UK: Pearson Education; Zinsser, W. 2012. *On Writing Well: The Classic Guide to Writing Non-Fiction* (30th Anniversary ed.). London, UK: HarperCollins.

[57] Bartunek, J. M., Rynes, S. L., & Ireland, R. D. 2006. What makes management research interesting, and why does it matter? *Academy of Management Journal*, 49: 9–15. Franklin, J. 1994. *Writing for Story: Craft Secrets of Dramatic Non-Fiction*. London, UK: Penguin.

or 3 journals, only to be accepted by the next one, if you have been improving it in the meantime. You're in it for the long haul. Scholarly papers take years to go through the review process of two or three cycles in a journal, before they are accepted and published. The process is longer if a paper is rejected in the second or third review cycles as opposed to being desk-rejected. This may occur because the reviewers and the editor do not see sufficient progress and contribution that responds to their concerns from earlier cycles; or it could happen sometimes when the editorial team of a journal changes and the new team does not see the same promise in a paper that the previous team saw.

When revising a manuscript, it is important to respond meticulously to the reviewers' and editor's concerns, and make it clear in your responses how you responded and where in the revised paper your changes may be found. Sometimes it may be necessary to explain to the reviewers in your responses any aspects of your theoretical framing and method that are novel and that the reviewers are unfamiliar with. Sometimes, reviewers may forget what they asked you to do in the previous review cycle, and may ask for something that is contradictory at a later stage. In this case, point this out objectively and politely.

It is important to frame your responses in a positive way, despite any frustration you may be experiencing with the review comments and requirements. The review process is also a social process and exhibiting frustration is unlikely to help reach an eventual positive outcome. It should be noted that in some cases, the time and energy levels invested to produce good replies to reviewers may approximate the levels invested in revisions to the actual manuscript.

The publication process of scientific work is a competitive endeavor. Journals have a limited number of pages, and their prestige is associated with the rejection rate of submitted manuscripts. At each stage of the revision process, your ideas and theoretical insights get tested by the peer review system and by editorial scrutiny. The process can be long and frustrating. Once your manuscript is accepted however, you can feel a sense of well-deserved accomplishment.

Your manuscript will face severe tests before (and if) it is eventually published

Some aspects of publication strategy

Given the limited tenure clock time, and the length of time it takes for a paper to be reviewed, it is important to go for concurrent rather than sequential submissions of the papers arising from your PhD. In other words, you will have to juggle several balls in the air simultaneously. If you submit your papers sequentially, after waiting for editorial decisions on one paper before you submit another paper, the likelihood is that you will not have sufficient publications by the time the tenure clock chimes.

Further, choose the journals to submit your paper carefully. Try to understand what kinds of papers, themes, and methodologies each journal publishes, and submit your work to a journal in which your work fits. Submitting your work to special issues is a good idea, as the publishing process is often more swift and timely than the usual journal cycles. It is important to aim high. Even if your paper is rejected, you can learn something from the process and from the feedback, that can help your paper succeed in another journal.

Another important aspect of publication strategy is to aim for publication synergies from your work. If you spend years on fieldwork just to submit one or two papers for example, then the level of synergies is pretty low. This does not mean slicing your data and submitting narrow papers to journals, or submitting papers that are similar to each other (these being questionable practices from a research ethics perspective). It does mean however seeing how you can maximize returns from a given data set or from familiarity with a certain literature. When submitting multiple manuscripts based on the same dataset, it would be important to ensure that these manuscripts are different from each other in terms of research questions, theoretical bases, constructs, theoretical implications and managerial implications. A "uniqueness analysis" can help to gauge these differences[58].

Even when you co-author, publishing involves dedicated, consistent, often lonely work

Such considerations show why it is helpful to work on publications with experienced scholars such as your doctoral advisor as they can offer insights based on accumulated experience. Since publishing is a craft, it can be learned by apprenticeship and learning from scholars who are adept at the process. The box below offers

---

[58] Kirkman, B. L. & Chen, G. 2011. Maximizing your data or data slicing? Recommendations for managing multiple submissions from the same dataset. *Management and Organization Review*, 7: 433-446.

some thoughts on co-publishing with your doctoral advisor.

> **Box 6.2. Co-publishing with your doctoral advisor**
>
> While writing a PhD is rewarding in itself, it is important to think ahead about co-publishing your research with your supervisor and later with other colleagues in the academic community. The foundations for co-publishing are built very early: in jointly developing research ideas, understanding one another's strengths and weaknesses, finding complementarities in knowledge and skills, and showing mutual respect and appreciation. Any such process is a long undertaking, with trial and error, and it requires patience to achieve the desired results. I recommend that you regularly take a bird's-eye view, reflect on this process, and think about what you can improve. This is particularly important if you engage in interdisciplinary research. Every new project is different and requires you to spontaneously collaborate, build bridges between different knowledge areas, and find new complementarities. Moreover, the objective of your project is often a moving target. You will start with a clear picture of what you want to achieve together, but then you realise that there are other, perhaps more worthwhile objectives. Be open-minded, and don't be worried when your collaboration pivots in such ways – in fact, this often makes the collaboration more fruitful and interesting. You will find that you are able to transfer some of your existing skills to new topic areas in very unexpected ways. Indeed, this is a similarity between entrepreneurs and academics.

> Entrepreneurs typically don't take their initial objective is given – instead, they evaluate their existing skills and resources and ask which new objectives they could achieve with their endowment. Be entrepreneurial in your collaborations with your supervisor and beyond. Also, focus your efforts so that you don't spread yourself too thinly. It is easy to go to conferences, to be inspired, and to initiate all kinds of collaborations. Keep this inspiration and enthusiasm but remember that effective collaborations take time.
>
> *Hossam Zeitoun is an Associate Professor of Behavioral Science at the University of Warwick*

Finally, it is important to feel truly interested and even passionate about what you are researching; otherwise a PhD and subsequent efforts to publish from it will be a long, painful process. This is why we should be asking novel and consequential research questions in the first place, that are worth spending time and energy to answer, rather than incremental, narrow questions whose answer in the bigger picture would not in the end matter much.

The objective of this book has been to offer you a brief, action-oriented guide of how to approach the long and complex enterprise of doing a doctorate. We hope that it can help you as you embark in this exciting and challenging endeavor.

APPENDIX
Further reflections on the Doctoral process

In the Appendix we include some more reflections from PhD students who have successfully completed their degree. These views from the trenches are useful to read because they are born out of experience of conducting a PhD. They contain many common learning points, that can help to signpost your own journey and can help you avoid making some of the most basic mistakes in the process.

> **Box A1. Tips on the process of conducting your PhD**
>
> Doing a PhD is like taking a rollercoaster ride – a four years rollercoaster ride with its highs and lows, and unexpected twists and turns. The PhD process is a challenging individual experience, and at times a solitary one but it is also incredibly rewarding if you stick with it. If I could go back to day one of my PhD and speak to myself, these are the five things is what I would say:
>
> 1. Time flies so invest your time wisely! With the prospect of having four years to complete a PhD, it may look like time is on your side and with that thought it's easy to procrastinate. But believe me, it goes by faster than you could imagine. It's important to dedicate time each week to progressing with your research, be it reading, writing or thinking. The PhD is a creative process and it takes time to develop your research ideas, so write down your ideas, thoughts, or any sparks

of inspiration you get from your readings early on. And don't underestimate the time and effort it takes to think through and develop your research. Try to work on it progressively, a little at a time over the duration of your PhD. Have key milestones each year that you work towards as a way of monitoring your progress. It will help you stay on top of your research and save you from the dangers that come with leaving things to the last minute. Your final PhD thesis doesn't have to be a perfect work of art. It is a work in progress and you will have the opportunity to develop your research further post the PhD.

2. Expect your research to change. Over time your research question can evolve and be reshaped because of your readings, research findings or other unexpected factors. Be flexible in your thinking, keep an open mind and don't think that the research ideas and questions you started with will necessarily be what you end with. Let your research objective direct your method of research – be it quantitative, qualitative or mixed methods. Being adaptable allows you to discover novel findings and contributions to knowledge. And remember inspiration can come from anywhere, anything and anyone.

3. Don't compare yourself. In working alongside other PhD researchers, it is easy to compare yourself and your research progress but resist the urge to do so. It doesn't help and only serves to create anxiety and worry. Your PhD research is different and so is the way you work. Figure out your own working style. Are you more productive early in the morning or a night owl? Do you prefer

to scribble your ideas or take a more structured approach? Do you work better from home, in an office or from another location? Find out what works best for you and focus on that.

4. Engage with your supervisors and invest in the relationship. The supervisor-supervisee relationship is different for each student, but it is an important one to maintain. Seek your supervisors' advice and expertise. They are a valued source of knowledge and care about your success. At times, there may be moments of conflict but always aim to resolve this and talk it through. This relationship goes beyond just the PhD, they can become your collaborators, and fellow colleagues.

5. And don't forget to live! The PhD is a big commitment and can consume your time, thinking space and even your social life. But it is important to take time out, relax (maybe find a new hobby, learn an instrument or take up a sport). And importantly stay connected to those in your network - your friends and family. They will be your biggest cheerleaders and a huge source of emotional support when things get tough (and in some cases even financially). On a personal level, life can throw you some curveballs during your PhD but take each day as it comes, rely on your support network, and remember there is light at the end of the tunnel!

Doreen Agyei completed her PhD on organizational ambidexterity at the University of Warwick in 2017

Box A2. Things I wish I knew before I started my PhD

1. Plan well and begin writing at the right time. Doing a PhD is a long, hard and enriching experience. What could be helpful is to set up deadlines. For instance, at the end of the year, I will have a first draft for this paper. Do not write straight away once you have the first results. You should take time to compare them with the literature, and discuss your findings with other scientists. It is better to have comments before putting everything together. At the same time, you should not wait too long before writing. Find the right moment. Leaving your paper aside for a while can be constructive. Sometimes, you do not know what to do anymore to improve one paper. It could be necessary to leave it for a while and to go back at it after. You could have a new vision, new ideas.

2. Present your work and interact with colleagues and professors. Present your work even if it is a work-in-progress. Once you have a first draft of your paper, do not hesitate to present it at conferences. It is always a good way to receive comments. It also helps you to meet other scientists working on the same topics. Networking is important. Discuss with your PhD colleagues and with professors. The more you talk about your work, the broader perspective you will have. We always miss something when working alone. Do not hesitate to talk with other scientists from your research team or from other places. For sure, they will always have something interesting to tell you, a new approach. A PhD candidate should not

only stay at their desk. It is important that you get involved in your laboratory life. Go to seminars, it would give you ideas to see other scientists presenting their own work even if they are not exactly working on the same topics. Organize seminars, it would help you to meet colleagues and it would give you some useful experience.

3. Create an opportunity to co-author a paper. Writing at least one paper by yourself is highly valued because it proves that you possess the needed skills. However, it is also enriching to co-author a paper. It is a completely different exercise.

4. Do not be shy to ask for help. If you are lost in you work, it is important to contact your supervisor or to discuss with others. Do not keep things for yourself. Otherwise, you will probably get depressed. You are not alone!

5. Start thinking about the next steps before the end of the PhD and prepare a job market paper. When completing your PhD in the very last months, you will probably have no time to look for another job. It is necessary that you start thinking about what you want to do beforehand. Do not hesitate to discuss with your colleagues and other members of your research team in order to define all the possible options and find the ones for you. Once you have a clearer idea, you should start having a look at job ads. If you want to pursue in the academic life, start thinking about a job market paper. If you want to stay in academics, you will probably need a job market paper. So, you should think about it when doing one chapter

of your thesis and design it in order to make it a job market paper afterwards.

Marine de Talancé completed her PhD in Economics at PSL Université Paris Dauphine

---

Box A3. Things I wish I knew before I started my PhD

1. Start teaching as soon as possible. teaching may seem difficult at the beginning, and it requires a significant amount of time but it gets easier with experience and you can benefit from the economies of scale if you teach the same course to different groups. So the sooner you start the faster you will adapt and the less time consuming it becomes in the future. Also, choose the courses you teach wisely: You need to make the most of your teaching experience as teaching is a great opportunity to learn as well.

2. Back up your computer often. having regular backups is crucial when you have the fruit of years of endeavor in one place. The life cycle of a computer is limited and a sudden breach may be more common than what you imagine. Besides having several backups can be a psychological relief.

3. Organize well everything that you read. A PhD is a long process, it is essential for you to be able to find a paper you have read at the beginning of your PhD journey anytime in the future. Also, write things down as soon as possible: Whenever you have a good idea take the time to write it down. It may be more difficult to find the best words when you force yourself to write a very long document in one go.

Personally I prefer to assemble a couple of well written texts together.

4. Get to know other researchers in the lab working on subjects similar to yours. it is always an asset to know someone who can give a second opinion about your research other than your supervisor. Also, discuss your research with your fellow PhD students: other PhD students (especially the older ones) can give you useful comments and advice and are likely to have faced the same struggles you are facing today. Finally, become part of different networks: Your supervisor may not know all the administrative details or offers. Make sure your email address is added to every mailing list and that you receive information about different interesting seminars in your field. Take regular lunch/coffee breaks with other researchers in your lab and discuss about the upcoming important events.

5. Think about publication possibility ex ante. once you have your problematic it is best to identify the potential journals for your future publications. Sometimes it is best to make minor changes too adapt your work to their scope in order to maximize your publication chances. This search in advance helps you to construct a comprehensive literature review.

6. Always have your final goals in mind. by the end of your PhD you need to have a well written job market paper and a network in your domain to find your ideal job. Keep those goals in mind and do not hesitate to contact people and present your work.

Yeganeh Forouheshfar completed her PhD in Economics at Université Paris Dauphine PSL in 2017.

Box A4. The roles of the PhD supervisor and of the PhD candidate from a student's perspective

The role of the PhD supervisor

Your PhD supervisor will be the cornerstone of your PhD thesis. As such, you could expect them to fulfill three essential roles.

1. First, to inform you and to help you to fit in your research team. Your PhD supervisor has a broad vision about the research community. They should therefore guide you in this world and explain in detail what is expected from you. Never underestimate the power of experience. Moreover, they are in the best position to introduce you to the other members of your research team and to help you to contact other researchers who work on your topics.

2. Second, to encourage you but also to provide useful insights. Completing a PhD thesis is not an easy task and you will for sure encounter some difficulties. Your PhD supervisor should help you to overcome them by giving you advice and by supporting you. However, they should also be critical and question your methods and your findings in order to help you to significantly improve your work.

3. Third, to give you deadlines and meet with you regularly. Writing a PhD thesis is a long exercise and sometimes you can get lost. That is why fixing regular meetings with your PhD supervisor could help you to progress and organize your work.

The role of the PhD candidate

As a PhD candidate, you are also expected to fulfill several roles.

1. First, you should be able to work independently. Of course your PhD supervisor is here to help you, but writing a PhD thesis is first of all a personal work. So before seeking support, you need to think by yourself, to clarify your ideas and look for answers. Often, they are not very hard to find.

2. Second, you should be curious. When working in academic research, you should always encourage your thirst for knowledge, maintain and develop your knowledge. This includes for instance attending conferences, seminars, reading articles, etc.

3. Third, you are expected to be serious and rigorous. Always take your work seriously and be organized. For instance, prepare carefully your meetings with your supervisor. Write down what you want to discuss and send your papers in advance so they can also prepare for these meetings.

4. Fourth, you should accept criticism and acknowledge the limits of your work. Writing a good article is an iterative process. You will have a first version and present it to your supervisors or in a conference where other researchers will have different visions and point out the limits of your work. This is a good thing, do not panic! Write down all the remarks, they will help you to improve significantly your work.

Marine de Talancé completed her PhD in Economics at Université Paris Dauphine PSL in 2017.

Printed in Great Britain
by Amazon